W

Preventing and Recovering from Date Rape

by
Josh McDowell

IT CAN HAPPEN TO YOU
Copyright © 1991 Josh McDowell

Scripture quotations are taken from:
The Holy Bible, New International Version, (NIV)
Copyright © 1973, 1978, 1984 by the International
Bible Society. Used by permission of Zondervan
Bible Publishers.

Indicated by (ICB): The Holy Bible, International
Children's Bible, New Century Version, Copyright
© 1983, 1986, 1988 by Word Publishing. Used by
permission of Word, Inc.

Indicated by (TLB): The Living Bible

Library of Congress Cataloging-in-Publication Data
McDowell, Josh.
    It can happen to you : what you need to know
about preventing and recovering from date rape /
by Josh McDowell.
        p.   cm.
    Includes bibliographical references.
    Summary: Explores the issue of date rape from
a Christian perspective, discussing how it can be
prevented and how its victims can get help,
begin the healing process, and recover.
    ISBN 0-8499-3291-2
    1. Acquaintance rape—United States. 2.
Acquaintance rape—United States—Prevention. [1. Acquaintance rape. 2. Rape.] I. Title.
HB6561.M27 1991
362.88'3—dc20   91-1973
                                        CIP
                                        AC

1 2 3 4 5 9   5 4 3 2 1

Printed in the United States of America

CONTENTS

— ACKNOWLEDGMENTS —

This book is the outgrowth of the pamphlet "It Happened to Me" and the "Date Rape" video production. I want to thank Victoria Kepler Didato, Dr. Berry Burkhart, Dr. Peg Zeigler, Dr. Dan Allender, Kevin Huggins, Kaye Malyuk, Dr. Norm Wakefield, and Gene Mack for their valuable input. But special thanks goes to Becky Bellis for her dedication and compassionate heart that reaches out to hurting people and for the initiative she took to help the sexually abused when she coordinated the writing of the "It Happened to Me" pamphlet. It was through Becky's vision as book writer/editor that also brought this publication into existence. Thanks also goes to Denise Bellis for her invaluable professional contribution and untold hours of work creating reams of research and background material; to Ed Stewart for his talented writing skills in refining the manuscript; to Jan Frank for incorporating her expert insights into the book upon reviewing the manuscript; to Sheri Livingston Neely for her additional input and for taking the manuscript through its final stages; and finally, to Dave Bellis, my Resource Development Director, for guiding this entire project to completion. This book has truly been a collaborative effort.

Josh McDowell

CHAPTER ONE

How Could This Happen to Me?

Jamie and Todd met at the Campbell College campus mixer in late September and dated through the fall term—mostly to football games and "fifth quarter" parties. Todd, a junior class officer, knew at first glance that Jamie was a freshman he wanted to know better. And Jamie was impressed by Todd's upper-classman sophistication. She was also thrilled to learn that Todd, too, was a Christian, and they began attending the campus fellowship group together. Just before Jamie left school for Christmas break, Todd kissed her for the first time.

During winter term Jamie and Todd studied and partied together, attended church and campus fellowship group activities together, and talked together about everything from current events to the Second Coming. When Jamie was with Todd, she felt cared for, protected, and loved. And being with such a warm, soft beauty like Jamie made Todd's head swim with excitement. Most of their evenings together concluded with about an hour of cozy cuddling in Todd's car outside Jamie's dorm. No doubt about it: Todd and Jamie were in love.

Campbell's Spring Formal was their first real "dress up" date in seven months together. Todd arrived at the dorm wearing a smart, conservative black tux, and Jamie was a vision of femininity as she greeted him in her elegant teal formal and silver jewelry. The handsome couple drove to the lakeside country club and danced the evening away starry-eyed.

They left at midnight, but instead of heading back to the college, Todd drove slowly along the shore to the far side of the lake and parked overlooking a secluded, moonlit cove. Their customary cuddling session heated up quickly in the romantic setting. In between kisses Todd slipped out of his jacket, unbuttoned his collar, and reclined both of their seats. "I love you, Jamie," he said softly, "and I've wanted to be with you like this for a long time." Then he began kissing and caressing Jamie more intimately than he had ever done before.

Jamie was hungry for Todd's affection, and part of her wanted him to continue. But another part of her realized that Todd was crossing the threshold of intimacy she had reserved for marriage. "I love you too, Todd," she whispered. "But I think we've had enough for tonight."

Todd didn't seem to hear her. His kissing and fondling became feverish and forceful. Jamie tried to push him away, but he was too strong for her. Suddenly she felt vulnerable and afraid in the presence of the man she loved and trusted. *This can't be happening to me,* she thought frantically. She tried to squirm away from Todd, but he had her pinned to her seat. "Stop, Todd; this isn't right!" she insisted, almost screaming. "I don't want to do this!" But Todd didn't stop.

Several minutes later Todd sat slumped over the steering wheel, dazed and silent with remorse. Jamie huddled in a corner of the back seat sobbing. Her beautiful gown was torn and stained, and her wrists and neck burned from Todd's powerful grip. *Why me, God?* she whimpered inside. *I've always been careful around strangers and maintained my standards on dates. How can something God created to be a wonderful expression of love be distorted into rape? What did I do wrong? What should I have done differently? What do I do now?*

If you look upon Todd and Jamie's experience as a tragedy, you're right. In a fit of unguarded passion, an apparently normal, red-blooded Christian young man became a rapist, and a young, innocent girl became a rape victim. Try as they may, Todd and Jamie will never forget this horrible night. Jamie's minor physical wounds will heal in a few days, but the emotional pain she suffered will take months—maybe years—to heal. And Todd may feel he will never be able to forgive himself for what he did.

But if you think something similar could never happen to you or to one of your friends, you're dead wrong. Jamie, Todd, and Campbell College are fictional, but what Todd did to Jamie in his car beside the moonlit cove is painfully realistic, especially to thousands of American women who have been the victims of date rape. Sexual aggression in acquaintance relationships—including date rape—is an all-too-frequent phenomenon today, especially on our college campuses.

How frequent? It's difficult to say exactly, because victims like Jamie are typically hesitant to report acts of sexual aggression, especially when the man involved is someone they know. But several major studies conducted over the last thirty years reveal that date rape and its related offenses are much more common in America than we would like to admit. For example, imagine that fictitious Campbell College is a typical American institution with two thousand students—a thousand men and a thousand women. If you apply the results of the most significant national studies to this small campus you will discover that:

- About eight hundred of the women at Campbell (that's eight in ten—80 percent!) have been victimized by some form of sexual aggression in their high school and college dating experiences. By sexual aggression I mean unwanted physical contact, sexual coercion, attempted rape, or rape. Women aged 16–19 are the most victimized group, and women aged 20–24 are a close second. The rate of victimization for these two groups is four times greater than the mean for all women.

- More than five hundred of Campbell's male students (50 percent) have perpetrated some form of sexual aggression in their high school and college dating experiences.

- Approximately two hundred and fifty women (one in four) have experienced attempted rape, and one hundred and twenty-five (one in eight) have been raped.

- About two hundred and fifty Campbell men (one in four) have forcefully attempted sexual intercourse against their dates' wishes. Despite the pleading, crying, screaming, and fighting from their dates, about one hundred and fifty of them, like Todd, succeeded.

- About one hundred of the hundred and twenty-five Campbell rape victims (80 percent) were with a close acquaintance or date, someone they have known an average of almost one year, when they were raped. Nearly half of these men were first dates, casual dates, or romantic acquaintances.

- More than one hundred of the hundred and twenty-five date rapes occurred off campus, half of them on the man's turf (his apartment, his car, and so forth). About sixty-five of the victims (over 50 percent) were raped during or at the end of a planned date.

You may be thinking, *those are interesting statistics, but date rape has never happened to me, and it never will. I'm a Christian. I have moral standards. The people I go out with are nice people. Why do I need to read a book on date rape?* In light of the previous figures, I have three answers to your question.

First, if you are a single woman between the ages of sixteen and twenty-four, you have an 80 percent chance of being victimized by some form of sexual aggression, including date rape.[1] And girls, *no* man you date—not even a Christian guy—comes with an iron-clad guarantee that he will never come on to you against your wishes. You are in the greatest danger of sexual assault and date rape when you think you are immune to them. Jamie asked herself too late, *What should I have done differently?* You need to understand date rape before it happens and do your best to prevent it from happening to you. This book will help equip you to do that.

Second, perhaps the scenario of Jamie and Todd is painfully familiar to you because you have already been personally involved in an incident of sexual aggression. Maybe you were the victim of rape or attempted rape by a man you dated or trusted. As a victim, your emotions have no doubt hit bottom hard: guilt, shame, anger, fear, despair. Your thoughts have raced from *It didn't happen to me* to *What do I do now?* and back again more times than you can count. For you, the worst has already happened, and you're hurting.

I've written this book not only to help people prevent date rape, but to help victims and perpetrators work through the emotional pain of date rape and begin the healing process. I want you to begin seeing yourself as a survivor—not just a victim—of what happened to you. I've included a number of steps to help you survive your experience.

Finally, since you undoubtedly have friends in your age group, you know many people who are potential date rape victims and perpetrators. As the old saying goes, there's safety in numbers. You and your friends need to talk with each other about the dangers of sexual aggression and hold each other accountable to avoid them. After all, that's what friends are for!

Or you may have a friend whose life is already scarred by an incident of sexual aggression. You haven't said much to her because you don't know what to say. Maybe you've even avoided her, thinking she somehow set herself up. Don't bail out on your friend now. She needs you more than ever. God may want to use you to lead your friend through the steps of healing that will transform her from a victim to a survivor. This book will help you do that.

Getting over a traumatic incident like date rape is a process, not an overnight quick-fix. But there is hope and healing for you. Thank you for letting me share it with you and your friends.

CHAPTER TWO

What Is Date Rape?

Imagine for a moment that you are a student at mythical Campbell College attending the Spring Formal at the country club by the lake. You can't help but notice the glow of love in Jamie and Todd's eyes as they cling to each other on the dance floor. Then about midnight, as you leave the country club to drive back to the college, you notice that Todd's car turns the other way—toward the dark, romantic side of the lake. You probably say to yourself, *I'm no rocket scientist, but I think I know what Todd and Jamie have on their minds.*

Now it's Monday noon, you are huddled with your friends around a table in the campus burger shop, and the topic of conversation is Todd and Jamie. "Did you see which way Todd's car was headed after the Spring Formal?" someone says. "I'll bet he and Jamie got pretty *in*formal on the far side of the lake." Everybody laughs that knowing laugh.

"Todd's apartment is in my complex, and he didn't get in until after three."

"Well, Jamie is in my dorm, and the word around our floor is that Todd got a little carried away with Jamie in the moonlight."

"That sly devil! But, like they say, it takes two to tango. I'll bet Jamie got a little carried away herself."

"Yeah, did you see her hanging all over Todd at the country club? Whatever Jamie got, she was asking for!"

What really happened in Todd's car that night at the lake? It seems that everybody around the table has an opinion, but nobody is using the "R" word. Is rape not really rape when it happens on a date? Is it excusable because the girl knows the guy, has dated him, or has even slept with him before? Are a guy's actions justified if his date was "asking for it" by dressing or acting seductively or by agreeing to "park"?

In order to help prevent date rape from happening to you and your friends, you need to understand what date rape is and what date rape isn't.

Date Rape IS Rape

When a man has sexual intercourse with a woman after she has communicated through her words and/or actions that she doesn't want it, he has committed rape. It doesn't matter if he is a stranger to her, an acquaintance, a friend, her lover, or her husband. It doesn't matter that she has allowed him to "park" with her. It doesn't matter that she may have consented to have sexual intercourse with him or another man in the past. It doesn't matter if she is sober and alert or drunk, stoned, or asleep. If his penis penetrates her vagina when she is unwilling or unable to give her consent, it's rape. If he tries to penetrate but is thwarted, it's attempted rape.

There are two categories of rape. The first can be called **stranger rape,** where the victim does not know her assailant. Stranger rapes, often accompanied by violence and sometimes even by murder, are the kinds you hear about on the eleven o'clock news. It's the fear of stranger rape that drives many women to take self-defense courses, install multiple door locks, buy pistols for the night stand, and carry Mace in their purses.

The second category is **acquaintance rape,** where the assailant is known by the victim in some way. He may be your neighbor, a classmate, a co-worker, your teacher, or a relative. He may be your roommate's brother, your boyfriend's best friend, or someone you met at a party. He may be someone you are dating casually or steadily or with whom you are romantically involved or physically intimate.

Acquaintance rape in a dating relationship is commonly referred to as **date rape**.

Date rape can be just as devastating as stranger rape, if not more so. The victim trusts her date to have her best interests at heart. She believes in him, assumes that he cares about her, and enjoys being with him. Her guard is down, and she is unprepared to resist his advances effectively. When he forces himself on her sexually, he violates her trust as well as her body. That's devastating!

You may be surprised to learn that acquaintance rapes greatly outnumber stranger rapes. One study conducted on thirty-two college campuses found that over 80 percent of the women who had been raped knew their attacker, and over 50 percent of the rapes occurred on dates![2] Yet you usually don't read about date rapes in the headlines, and you may not even hear about them when they happen to someone you know. Acquaintance rape and date rape are often referred to as "hidden rape." Why? Because many women who are raped by men they know don't think of it as rape. Some may think, "It was my fault; I led him on" or "I should have said 'no' more forcefully." And most offenders who end up raping their date don't view themselves as rapists. They may say, "It was a mistake" or "Sure she *said* 'no,' but I know she didn't mean it" or "I got a little carried away" or "She made me lose control." And the closer the man and woman are to each other, the less serious the rape is judged, even by their friends. In our minds, the term "rape" applies only to hideous scenes like women being abducted from parking lots at gunpoint, dragged into the woods, and repeatedly assaulted by crazed, pathological criminals. But make no mistake: **Rape is rape, even when it is perpetrated by someone you know, love, and trust.**

Date Rape Is a Crime

If Todd had pulled a gun on Jamie after the rape, taken her money, and fled, she could have had him arrested for robbery. If he had beaten her up in the process, assault and possibly attempted murder could have been added to the charges. But since he "only" raped her, it's likely that Jamie will never report the incident to campus security, a rape crisis center, a physician, or the police. Women who have been raped by men they know often fail to see themselves as victims of a crime.

But the law is clear: Unwanted sexual intercourse—even when perpetrated by an acquaintance, date, or husband—is a felony punishable by imprisonment. Yet rape is the most underreported of all felonies. Government agencies estimate that three to ten rapes actually occur for every one rape reported to police.[3] One study revealed that only 5 percent of over fifteen hundred women who were victims of rape or attempted rape in college ever reported the crime to law enforcement or college authorities.[4] Other experts estimate that at the most, half—and possibly only 10 percent—of all rapes are reported to the police.[5]

Why aren't rapes reported? Primarily because many rape victims don't acknowledge it as a crime. In a study of nearly five hundred women who were victims of incidents that met the legal definition of rape, only 23 percent of them considered it rape and 62 percent did not view it as *any* kind of crime.[6]

Why is our society so soft on rape as a crime? At least part of the answer may be found in the media. Today's television programs, movies, and pulp novels glorify illicit sex and, except in rare situations, whitewash sex crimes such as rape.

Take the soaps for example. In his article, "A Plea to the Soaps: Let's Stop Turning Rapists into Heroes" (*TV Guide*, May 27, 1989), writer Gerard Waggett cites a number of incidents from a decade of soap opera episodes which make rapists look like misguided but forgivable romantics instead of criminals:

- *General Hospital*: Luke raped Laura, but instead of naming Luke as her assailant, Laura eventually fell in love with him and married him. At one point she even referred to the rape as "the first time we made love"! Although the plot outraged many viewers, critics, and women's groups, it was so popular that Luke became the leading character in the show and actor Anthony Geary (Luke) became a media sex symbol.

- *Ryan's Hope*: Roger failed in his attempt to force his ex-lover Maggie into bed, but succeeded in marrying her two years later.

- *Dynasty*: Adam raped Kirby one season and proposed to her the next.

- *All My Children*: Ross raped Natalie in a drunken, vengeful rage. Natalie pressed charges, and Ross went to prison. But he broke out to rescue his adopted daughter and became a hero.

- *As the World Turns*: Josh raped his cousin (by adoption) Iva when they were teenagers, and she bore his daughter. After learning he was a father, Josh regretted his past and accepted his role as the girl's father. But then he paired up with Iva's sister Meg. Iva and her mother accepted the relationship, in effect condoning the rape.[7]

Don't be fooled by media myths or popular opinion. Rape is not a mistake which can be legitimized if the offender eventually marries the victim. Rape is a crime. Rapists are not heroes in the rough; they're dangerous criminals who need to be punished and rehabilitated for their crimes.

Date Rape Is a Power Issue, Not a Sex Issue

Many people say that men like Todd force themselves on victims like Jamie because they are sex fiends whose desires are out of control. That's not really the case. Many significant studies have shown that rapists—including acquaintance rapists—act in response to three identifiable attitudes embedded in their personality which arm them as walking time bombs of sexual aggression:

The "I am the king" attitude. Show me a man who strongly believes in male dominance and female subservience, and I'll show you a potential rapist. This man has oversubscribed to the traditional male role. He accepts as truth the idea that a woman will only respect a man who will "lay down the law" for her. He believes that a man must show a woman who's boss or he'll end up hen-pecked. This man does not rape because he is hungry for sex, but because he is hungry for power. His passion is to control and conquer women, whom he sees as his adversaries for superiority. And if this man buys into the use of force, hostility, and even violence to express his dominance, he's even more likely to hurt and humiliate women in his sexual encounters.

The "act now, think later" attitude. Men who commit rape characteristically score very low on personal responsibility. They charge recklessly into situations without pausing to consider the consequences of their behavior. They follow their whims and urges instead of exercising self-discipline and restraint. They can become sexually aggressive tonight without thinking how they will explain their behavior tomorrow or deal with the obvious legal and emotional consequences they may face for months or years to come.

The "who cares about you?" attitude. Men who are prone to rape usually lack social conscience. They act for themselves with little regard for the feelings and well-being of others. "If you get in my way and get hurt," they reason, "that's your tough luck." In a sexual encounter they may be oblivious to the physical and emotional pain they are inflicting on their victim in the process of getting what they want.

These three attitudes are usually not very obvious in men who are prone to rape. If they were, these men would have a hard time even getting close to a woman, let alone dating one! Yet studies have shown that these tendencies hide beneath the surface of a surprising number of "normal" men who have admitted on surveys that they would rape if they could be assured of not being caught and punished.

Date Rape Is the Product of Male Sex Myths

The man who fits the three-fold profile of a potential rapist also buys into a number of male sex myths which he consciously or subconsciously uses to legitimize his sexual aggression. Here are several of the myths that are in circulation today:

Women really want to be raped. This myth is an extension of the attitude of male dominance mentioned above. "Entertainment" media often condition men to look at women as objects to be raped, as beings whose sole worth is in their sexual stimulus. Men who accept this myth believe that women enjoy being dominated, including sexually. Women get turned on when men play rough. When a woman says no, she doesn't really mean it. If she did, she could make him stop because no woman can be raped against her will. It's all part of the game. Subconsciously, she really wants to be conquered.

That's a myth! No woman welcomes sexual victimization.

Women owe sex to men who spend money on them. A survey of junior high students revealed that this myth has even infected the younger generation. In the survey, 51 percent of the boys and 41 percent of the girls said a man has a right to force a woman to kiss him if he has spent a lot of money on her. Twenty-five percent of the boys and 17 percent of the girls said forced sex is okay if the man has spent money on her.[8] As one man said, "I don't expect to take a woman out, spend a lot of money on her, and then drive home alone. Sex should be part of most evenings."

That's crazy! Any money a guy spends on a girl is a gift. If he attaches strings to it, she should pay her own way or forget the relationship.

Women can control themselves sexually; men can't. Many men claim that they can only "make out" so long before they "cross the line" and lose control of their sex drive. At that point they're not responsible for their actions. In other words, it is unrealistic to wait because their libido (sex drive) is too strong. In fact, the guy will often blame the girl for an act of date rape because it was her fault for taking him over the line.

That's another myth. A man has as much control over his sexual behavior as he does over his eating habits. How a man (or a woman) responds to his sex drive is his choice, not an uncontrollable knee-jerk reaction.

Women may say no, but their actions say yes. A lot of men claim that women dress and act seductively in order to turn guys on. When a woman resists his attempts at sex, a man may say, "You tell me to stop, but everything else you do says go. You dress in sexy outfits. You send me those flirty looks across the room. You cuddle with me in the car. I know you're playing hard-to-get with me; that's what girls are supposed to do. I'm only giving you what you really want."

In most cases these men are reading messages that women aren't sending. Women usually dress and behave for personal satisfaction and social acceptance, not to interest men in sex. Yet men tend to perceive life in sexual terms. So a man may misinterpret a woman's stylish, flattering outfit as a billboard advertising her sexual availability. And he may regard every good-night kiss or cuddle in the moonlight as merely a preliminary to the "main event."

Studies show that men tend to see a woman's friendliness as an interest in sex. Therefore a man may *overrate* a woman's expressions of friendship and *underrate* her verbal protests to his sexual advances. But no matter what a woman's nonverbal messages may suggest, it's likely that when she *says* no, she *means* no.

If the woman's not a virgin, it's not rape. Nearly one-third of the junior high students surveyed saw nothing wrong with raping a woman who was already sexually active.[9] This response reflects another male myth which dismisses the rape of a non-virgin with, "No harm was done; she was already a 'bad girl'" Yet no matter how active a woman may be sexually, forcing sexual intercourse on her is rape.

Date Rape Is Violent

Men who will violate a woman sexually have the potential to violate her physically and even kill her. One woman said after her sister had been murdered by a former boyfriend, "It's hard to believe even after it happened that a woman could lose her life because she rejected a man." Yet many women and girls are murdered every year attempting to resist sexual aggression.

One study found that 87 percent of rapists either carry weapons or threaten violence or death.[10] In another study of college women who had experienced sexual aggression, various levels of violence were experienced. Forty-eight percent of the offenders simply ignored the victim's protests and requests to stop. Thirty-two percent verbally coerced their victims into the offensive or displeasing event. Fifteen percent used physical restraint, and 6 percent used various kinds of threats or physical aggression.[11]

Marge Piercy expressed the chilling reality of rape violence in the following poem:

> There is no difference between being raped
> and being pushed down a flight of
> cement steps
> except that the wounds also bleed inside.
>
> There is no difference between being raped
> and being run over by a truck
> except that afterward men ask if you
> enjoyed it.
>
> There is no difference between being raped
> and being bit on the ankle by a rattlesnake
> except that people ask if your skirt was short
> and why you were out alone anyhow.
>
> There is no difference between being raped
> and going head-first through a windshield
> except that afterward you are afraid
> not of cars, but half the human race. . . .[12]

Date Rape Is Against God's Plan

There are a lot of topics in the Bible which are open to different interpretations, but proper sexual behavior isn't one of them. God clearly designed sex to be enjoyed by a man and a woman in a loving, committed, monogamous relationship. Any attitude or action which departs from God's standard is sexual immorality, as the following verses declare:

- You shall not commit adultery (Exodus 20:14).

- Do not lust in your heart after [the immoral woman's] beauty or let her captivate you with her eyes (Proverbs 6:25).

- You have heard that it was said, "Do not commit adultery." But I tell you that anyone who looks at a woman lustfully has already committed adultery with her in his heart (Matthew 5:27–28).

- Do not be deceived: Neither the sexually immoral nor idolaters nor male prostitutes nor homosexual offenders . . . will inherit the kingdom of God. . . . Flee sexual immorality (1 Corinthians 6:9–10, 18).

- But among you there must not be even a hint of sexual immorality, or of any kind of impurity (Ephesians 5:3).

- Put to death, therefore, whatever belongs to your earthly nature: sexual immorality, impurity, lust, evil desires (Colossians 3:5).

- It is God's will that you should be holy; that you should avoid sexual immorality (1 Thessalonians 4:3).

- Marriage should be honored by all, and the marriage bed kept pure, for God will judge the adulterer and all the sexually immoral (Hebrews 13:4).

In addition to going against God's guidelines for sexual purity, date rape violates God's supreme law: the law of love. The primary word for love in the New Testament is *agape*. *Agape* love is the purest form of love. It's an unselfish love, a giving love. *Agape* is the opposite of the lust for power and sex which motivates rape. Lust reaches out to grab what it wants; love reaches out to give what others need.

Only a fool could miss the emphasis on unselfish love in the New Testament. Notice in these verses how God's law of love leaves no room for the selfishness of date rape:

- Jesus taught: "A new command I give you: Love one another. . . . By this all men will know that you are my disciples, if you love one another. . . .

Greater love has no one than this, that he lay down his life for his friends" (John 13:35–36, 15:13).

- Paul wrote: "Be devoted to one another in brotherly love. Honor one another above yourselves. . . . The commandments, 'Do not commit adultery,' 'Do not murder,' 'Do not steal,' 'Do not covet,' and whatever other commandment there may be, are summed up in this one rule: 'Love your neighbor as yourself'" (Romans 12:10, 13:9).

- Peter wrote: "Now that you have purified yourselves by obeying the truth so that you have sincere love for your brothers, love one another deeply, from the heart" (1 Peter 1:22).

- And John wrote: "Dear friends, let us love one another, for love comes from God. Everyone who loves has been born of God and knows God" (1 John 4:7).

Date Rape Is Criminal, Hurtful, and Immoral

In the next chapter, I want to share with you some specific and practical steps you can take to help keep date rape from happening to you and your friends.

CHAPTER THREE

How Can I Help Prevent Date Rape?

Two of the questions Jamie asked herself moments after being date raped by Todd were, "What did I do wrong?" and "What should I have done differently?" Good questions. Unfortunately for Jamie, she was asking them *after* being victimized.

Todd probably asked himself similar questions. True, he had been fantasizing for weeks about taking Jamie to the far side of the lake after the formal. He knew it was wrong, but he wanted to be with her like never before, and he was hoping she would cooperate. He was sure she was ready to go "all the way." But when Jamie resisted, he persisted. For reasons he still doesn't fully understand, Todd had to convince Jamie that he was her man. But on the long, silent ride back to Jamie's dorm, he seriously began to question his actions and motives.

Unfortunately, it was already too late for Jamie and Todd. The truth is that the best time to talk about avoiding date rape is long before you get involved in it.

Date Rape Can Happen—Even to Christians

Sexual abuse and assault is ugly. It can happen to you in so many ways. Someone could indecently expose himself to you. You could receive an obscene phone call. You could be the victim of a peeping Tom. As a child you can be sexually molested or assaulted by a relative (incest), a teacher, a neighbor, or a stranger. As an adult you can be sexually assaulted or raped by an acquaintance or a stranger. As Christians we may be equipped to make better life choices and to deal with life's tragedies, but we're not immune to sex crimes—either as victims or perpetrators—any more than we are immune to auto accidents or heart attacks.

There's only one way I know to avoid all sexual assault. Lock yourself in your house, don't let anyone in, and never go out. Even though it may seem fool-proof, it's not very practical, and I don't recommend it. We can't shut down our daily schedules and relationships just because date rape is a real and present danger. But there are some practical steps you can take to greatly minimize the chances that you will become a date rape victim. And there are some steps guys can employ to help them avoid the pitfalls that have turned other guys into date rapists. I want to share these steps with you.

For Girls

1. Set your limits and communicate them. Don't wait too long in a dating relationship to decide how far you'll go with a guy. If you do, your emotions may make a hasty decision in the back seat of a car that you will later regret. And if you wait too long to communicate your limits, a sexually aggressive man may overrule your decision in a moment of passion.

God's plan is that you save yourself sexually for the man you marry. That includes not only intercourse, but many of the sexually arousing activities that lead up to it (heavy petting, fondling of breasts and genitals, and so forth). One study determined that about 70 percent of all victims of rape or attempted rape have consented to some form of sexual activity on other occasions.[13] By contrast, a national survey of college women revealed that the *least* sexually victimized group was the one with the fewest sexual partners.[14] If you don't invite sexual activity, it's less likely that someone will force you into it.

I encourage you to make the decision to save sex for marriage. Include in your decision where you draw the line for dating. For example, you may decide that hand-holding is in but fondling is out, a good night kiss is okay but prolonged, deep kissing is not. Put your decision in writing where you will see it often (in your diary, your Bible, on your closet door). Then anchor your decision by telling someone who will support you in it and hold you accountable for it (your parents, a trusted friend, your pastor).

In your dating relationships, communicate your decision clearly. I'm not saying that you must greet every date at the door by reading him his "rights." But be ready to verbalize "this is okay" and "this is not okay" at the appropriate time. The book *Dating: Picking and Being a Winner*, published by Here's Life Publishers, can help you with this.

2. Avoid men who exhibit male myth characteristics. In chapter 2 I shared with you a profile of the kind of men who are most likely to become sexually aggressive. Keep as much distance between you and these men as possible. When they ask you out, say, "No, thank you," and walk away. How will you recognize a potential date rapist? There are a number of tell-tale signs:

- He emotionally abuses you by insulting you, belittling you, never listening to you, ignoring your opinions, or getting upset whenever you take the lead in the relationship.

- He refuses to let you share in the decisions or expenses of a date. He gets angry if you suggest an activity or offer to pay. He insists on being in charge of the relationship.

- He fails to treat you as an equal, flaunting that he is either older, smarter, bigger, stronger, or socially superior. He accepts the I-am-king-you-are-doormat view of sexual roles. He talks negatively about women in general.

- He mistreats you and others physically by pushing, pulling, grabbing, hitting, pinning you down, and so forth, even when it's disguised as play. He is overly forceful and controlling when making out. He enjoys being cruel to animals, children, or people he can bully. He is fascinated with weapons.

- He intimidates you by sitting too close, violating your physical or emotional space, using his body to block your way, touching you when you tell him not to, staring you down, or assuming a level of physical or emotional intimacy that makes you uncomfortable.

• He bosses you around and tries to control you by telling you how to dress, what you should do, who you should be friends with, and so on. He is easily angered by sexual and emotional frustrations. He gets jealous for no reason.

No matter how attractive they may seem to you, men who fit this description don't have your best interests at heart. They are domineering and irresponsible. They are the kinds of men who become rapists. If one of them gets on your trail, identify him to your friends and stay away from him. If he threatens you or abuses you in any way, talk to campus security or the police.

3. Learn to say no and mean it. Don't accept the cultural stereotype of women as passive, submissive doormats to men. You have the right to state what you want and don't want in a dating relationship. You don't owe a man sexual favors for spending money on you or for showing you a good time. You don't owe him sex when he claims you're responsible for turning him on.

Be assertive. Defend your limits by saying no in your actions, as well as by what you say. You can do this by facing him, looking him straight in the eyes and in a firm voice say, "No, I do not want to do this. You need to leave now." Don't be apologetic or wavering afterward by kissing him or caressing him as if to say, "I'm sorry." If you waver in this way, he may think you are saying "maybe," instead of "no." To help you learn to be definitive and assertive when you say no, it may help to practice in front of a mirror until it feels natural for you.

If he persists, push him away, get out of the car, walk out of the movie—do whatever you must to get out of an offensive setting. Always let a friend or your parents know where you will be in case you need to call them for a ride home.

4. Avoid excessive amounts of one-on-one time. According to college surveys, "parking" is the activity most strongly associated with sexual aggression. When you spend excessive amounts of unprogrammed time alone with a man in his car, in his apartment or yours, or in isolated locations (a secluded beach, the far side of the lake, a deserted park)—especially at night, you are asking for trouble. Some men think that if you're willing to be alone with them like this, you're interested in sex. Eliminate that possibility by encouraging double dates and group activities. Set a curfew for yourself by stating that you need to be in an hour after the activity is over. For example, if the movie ends at 9:45, tell your date to have you home by 10:45. That allows enough time to get a Coke, to talk a while, and to drive home. It also puts a lid on any plans he might have to take you to Inspiration Point after the movie "to watch the submarine races."

5.   Be aware of unintentional messages. Unfortunately, your actions may be misunderstood. Dress and act in harmony with your decision to avoid sex. Many women seek emotional closeness. They get this through conversation, sharing goals or dreams, and with appropriate touching. But often men confuse her desire to be emotionally close with sexual closeness.

It seems that God has created men and women with different levels of sexual arousal. Many men say they become aroused first by things they see, while many women say they become aroused first by touch. Therefore when a woman dresses in a pretty or sexy fashion, a man may think she's saying, "I want sex." But what the woman may really be saying is, "Please admire me." She probably is not thinking that he is becoming aroused sexually because of what she is wearing. So be alert to these differing perspectives and how they may be affecting your partner.

6.   Say no to alcohol and drugs. About 75 percent of the men and 55 percent of the women involved in acquaintance rape are under the influence of alcohol or drugs at the time of the assault.[15] Intoxicating substances reduce a man's inhibitions against sexual violence and limit a woman's ability to resist and defend herself. Stay away from these substances yourself, and stay away from the men who use them.

7. **Avoid blind dates.** Date only persons you know. Spend time becoming friends with a man before you go out with him. Let him get to know you as a person, and he will be less likely to view you as a sex object.

8. **Trust your instincts.** If you don't feel right about being with the guy who is asking you out or by doing what he wants to do, turn him down. If it *feels* wrong, it probably *is* wrong.

9. **Use wisdom and common sense.** Here are several suggestions which may help you avoid becoming the target of a stranger or acquaintance rapist:

- Think twice about giving your address or telephone number to people you don't know well.

- Keep your home well lit inside and out at night, and keep your curtains and shades drawn.

- Whenever you suspect a prowler, turn on all outside lights, call the police, and alert your neighbors.

- Positively identify all visitors before opening the door.

- Use deadbolt locks on the door, not chain locks. Lock all doors and windows when you are away.

- Keep your car doors locked and windows rolled up when driving in traffic. Be alert to the location of the nearest police station, fire station, or twenty-four-hour business. If you discover you're being followed, drive to one of these locations and honk your horn until you attract attention.

- If your car breaks down or runs out of gas, raise the hood, then get back inside, lock the doors, and wait for the police. If a man stops to offer help, ask him to call the police or the nearest service station.

- Never pick up hitchhikers, male or female.

- Always park your car in well-lighted areas, and lock it when you leave, even if for a short time.

- When walking, plan your route through well-traveled areas. Don't walk alone if you can avoid it. Don't accept rides from strangers, and never hitchhike.

- Hang up immediately on obscene phone calls.

- Don't volunteer information on the phone or tell people you are alone unless you know them very well.

- If you feel the atmosphere or conversation becoming sexually-oriented, try to change the mood or the subject of conversation.

- Listen to your friends. They may have heard "gossip" or tales of your date's previous experiences. Keep their warnings in mind when you are deciding where to go and what to do on a date with the man.

- Don't be afraid of offending your date by being firm. If he gets angry because you refuse to go to a certain location or don't want to continue necking if things are getting heavy, then you're better off saying good-bye and keeping your self-respect.

10. Appreciate a man who respects you. When you find a guy who listens to what you want in the relationship and respects your decisions about sex, tell him that you appreciate him for it. But be careful not to let your appreciation for him cause you to relax your standards.

For Guys

Some of the steps I've listed for girls also apply to a guy's role in dating relationships. First, it's just as important for him to set his sexual limits according to biblical guidelines and stick by them faithfully. It's his responsibility, not hers, to keep his drives under control. Second, he should take the lead in avoiding excessive amounts of one-on-one time. A guy should make plans to include others in dating activities, and he must learn to resist the temptation to spend time parking or making out. Third, he should stay away from alcohol and drugs. They can ruin his life as well as hers.

In addition, here are a few specific reminders and guidelines especially for guys:

1. Realize that it is never okay to force a girl to have sex. It doesn't matter how much money you've spent on her, how long you've been going out with her, or how much she apparently "wants it." It doesn't matter how many of your friends are doing it or how it is glorified in the media. Sexual intercourse outside of marriage, including date rape, is wrong.

2. Stop what you're doing when she says no. Your date's limits may be more conservative than yours, but when she says no to what you are doing or suggesting, honor her request. For example, you may be ready to move from a friendly brother-and-

sister-type peck on the lips to a romantic
embrace and tender kiss. But if she resists,
back off. Don't ask her if she really means no.
Don't pester her to change her mind. Respect her limits and stay within them.

**3. Avoid the stereotype of the domi-
nant, aggressive male.** The negative male
attitudes mentioned in the last chapter—"I
am the king," "Act now, think later," and
"Who cares about you?"—give rise to the
myths which condone sexual aggression and
rape. Don't allow yourself to get tricked into
this way of thinking. Instead, in your treatment of women, align your attitude with
scriptural guidelines. For example:

We are equals in God's sight. It's true that
the Bible lays down different principles for
husbands and wives in a marriage. Ephesians
5:22–33 is a prime example. But the difference in roles doesn't imply a difference in
importance between men and women. To
make this clear, the apostle Paul began his
explanation of roles by instructing, "Submit
to one another out of reverence to Christ"
(Ephesians 5:21). He also wrote in Galatians
3:28, "There is neither Jew nor Greek, slave
nor free, male nor female, for you are all one
in Christ Jesus."

As a man, you will have different
God-given responsibilities in your future relationship with your wife. But
then as now, God sees you as *equal*—not

superior—to the women in your life. Treat them accordingly.

Think first, act later. Your behavior is not under the control of your feelings and urges as some of the male myths suggest. Your actions are primarily controlled by your thoughts. Therefore, if you are going to rise above the stereotype of the desire-driven male, you need to gain control of your thought life. Paul wrote, "We take captive every thought to make it obedient to Christ" (2 Corinthians 10:5). When tempting thoughts demand that you throw caution to the wind, ignore your standards, and do what feels best, stop to think. Capture those thoughts and make them obedient to Christ first, then act.

I care about you. You will successfully avoid the dominant male stereotype in your thinking if you continually keep your date's best interests at heart. Paul instructed believers, "Do nothing out of selfish ambition or vain conceit, but in humility consider others better than yourselves" (Philippians 2:3). This guideline applies as much to dating as to any other relationship. If you make it your purpose always to treat your dates with honor, respect, and care, you will go a long way toward preventing date rape from happening in your relationships.

4. Keep your eyes from wandering. What you allow yourself to look at greatly affects your attitudes and behavior. Do you read pornographic magazines or books? Do you watch movies, videos, or television programs which contain scenes of nudity or sexual activity? The more you fill your eyes and your mind with material which degrades women and opposes God's standards of purity, the more you will be influenced to think and behave that way. Job's commitment to purity is a good model for Christian men today: "I made a covenant with my eyes not to look lustfully at a girl" (Job 31:1). I realize that Job didn't have to deal with the pornographic media blitz which surrounds us today. But a commitment to keep your eyes from wandering will help keep your mind and actions from wandering also.

Dealing with a Surprise Assault

Girls, suppose you have tried to be cautious with the man you are dating. But one night you are alone with him, and you suddenly realize that he intends to force you into sexual intercourse. You have repeatedly said no, but he ignores your resistance. What do you do now?

Rape experts suggest several steps of action to take in this setting:

1. **Stay calm.** Surveys show that women who avoided being raped had a lower emotional response to the initial attack. They felt less fear, self-blame, helplessness, and shock

when accosted than did the women who were raped. You need to keep your emotions under control and concentrate on being assertive.

2. Act quickly. Don't wait for your attacker to gain momentum. Don't think, *Maybe he will stop if I reason with him*. If he has ignored your pleas to stop, he is no longer your friend. He's an attacker capable not only of raping you but hurting you in other ways. Decide on a plan of action and start moving immediately.

3. Run away. If possible, bolt from his grasp and run for help. Run toward lights, buildings, the street—anywhere you're likely to find other people. If you're in a car, get out. If you can't get out, use the horn to attract attention.

4. Scream for help. If you can't get away and run, scream. It will immediately alert anyone nearby that you are in trouble. It may also surprise your attacker and allow you to get free and run.

5. Attack. If necessary, look for a way to hurt him physically in order to help you get away. If he is already exposed, his genital area is his most sensitive and his most debilitating. Be aware that he may respond to your attack with further violence, so make your first shot your best shot.

6. Buy time. If it appears that you are unable to get away or attract attention, try to talk your attacker out of his actions. Talk about God's displeasure with immorality. Talk about the legal charges he will face for going through with his plans. Talk about the social implications of his actions: his parents and other relatives will be ashamed of him, his friends will turn away from him, and so on. He may relax his guard as you talk, allowing you an opportunity to get away.

7. If your life is threatened. You may become aware that you are in a life-threatening situation. As a last resort, some women have survived only by giving in to his demands. This does not mean that you are consenting to have intercourse with him, but rather, you are choosing to save yourself from further harm by permitting him to do what he is going to do anyway. It is no less rape if you give in than if you resist until he seriously hurts you or kills you.

To this point in the book we have been talking about ways you can help prevent date rape from happening to you and your friends. But, unfortunately, sometimes our best preventative efforts fall short. Maybe you know someone who has already been sexually victimized. Maybe it's even happened to you. In the next two chapters we'll talk about the hope and healing which is available to the victims of sexual aggression and date rape.

CHAPTER FOUR

What Happens If I Am Date Raped?

Put yourself in Jamie's shoes for a moment. For more than six months you've been caught up in the excitement of being with Todd. Life has been wonderful knowing that someone as nice and as important as Todd loves you. He's good-looking, he's strong, he's smart, and he's a Christian. Sure, he's a little domineering, but you tend to overlook it because of his other qualities. You can't deny that you've thought about marriage a few times, almost hoping that Todd is the one for you.

Then comes the Spring Formal and the incident on the far side of the lake. Suddenly your beautiful relationship disintegrates, ground to powder by Todd's selfish passion. How do you feel? How are you dealing with a life turned upside down?

Maybe you don't need to put yourself in Jamie's shoes. Maybe you've been there yourself as the victim of date rape. You know all about the tormenting thoughts and feelings. You're still dealing with the physical, emotional, social, and spiritual fallout of that terrible event.

If this is what you are going through, you're experiencing what rape counselors call *rape trauma syndrome*. It's that bundle of emotional reactions to sexual assault which has become somewhat predictable in victims: shock, disbelief, embarrassment, shame, guilt, depression, powerlessness, disorientation, denial, fear, anxiety, and anger. Not only that, rape trauma syndrome also relates to a number of psychological, physical, social, and spiritual problems victims experience.

The first step to becoming a survivor of date rape is to understand what has happened to you—not just the rape itself, but all the turmoil it has brought to your life in the weeks, months, or even years since it happened. If you've been date raped, you need to know that most of your thoughts, feelings, and responses to the experience are normal. You also will be happy to learn that the turmoil you have experienced doesn't have to last forever. There is a way out. In this chapter I'd like to share with you the impact of date rape on a woman's life, and in the next chapter we'll talk about the process of healing. These concepts will be helpful to you if you are a date rape victim or if you are helping a friend who was a victim.

Physical Responses to Date Rape

For many victims, the most immediate and noticeable impact of date rape is physical. Some women report that their bodies are sore all over. Others say that certain areas ache more than other areas because of the focus of the assailant's force, such as the neck and throat, chest, ribs, arms and legs, pelvis, or genital area. Other women complain of loosened teeth, bruises, and abrasions suffered from either the attack or their attempts to escape. Some victims report that their sleep is affected, especially if the attack happened at night or in their own bed. They have difficulty falling asleep. They sometimes wake up screaming, tormented by recurring nightmares of the attack, and are unable to get back to sleep. Other victims experience a disturbance in their eating patterns as a result of sexual assault. Some victims have reported feeling self-hatred causing them to abhor their body. When this happens, other problems come into play which could include: a decrease in appetite, which may lead to compulsive disorders like over-eating, bulimia (binge eating and self-induced vomiting), or anorexia (self-starvation).

You may find that you struggle with other compulsive physical behaviors, such as compulsive exercising, perfectionism, house-cleaning, over-achieving, drug abuse, and so forth. Some women battle with extreme sexual attitudes or tendencies. Many also suffer from migraine headaches or stomach problems.

If you are the survivor of date rape, your body has suffered a tremendous shock. The way you respond physically to what happened to you reflects your body's attempts to cope with this shock. But there is hope for recovery as you allow God to walk with you through the healing process.

Emotional Responses to Date Rape

There are a number of different emotional responses which may accompany your experience of date rape. You may have suffered from some or all of them at one time or another. We will talk about a few of them here. However, don't be surprised if you struggle with some emotions we don't mention.

"I've lost something that I can never get back." There are a number of losses victims feel. Perhaps the rapist had been a trusted friend, but now the victim struggles with the fact that she's been betrayed and wonders if she can ever trust again. Victims struggle because of a loss of self-esteem—questioning their value and importantance to others. And, last but not least, there's the fact that if the victim was a virgin that physically she has lost something that she had been saving for the one she would someday marry.

With all of the losses that accompany date rape, a period of grieving should be expected. There are steps you can take to bring your perpetrator into account—such as legal action, church discipline, and so forth. But what you don't want to do is allow yourself to be crippled with a "get even" spirit. Allow God to do His work here too. Memorize Nahum 1:2, "God is jealous over those he loves; that is why *he* takes vengeance on those who hurt them" (TLB, emphasis mine). Repeat this verse to yourself whenever you are tempted to take revenge. Be careful not to confuse justice and accountability with revenge. Taking legal action is not the same as taking revenge. Revenge is when you scheme to harm the person who hurt you. Justice and accountability are when you take action that could prevent the perpetrator from harming someone else in the same way.

"It's my own fault." One of the most pervasive emotional responses to date rape is guilt. Victims feel partially responsible for what happened to them. They are plagued by a string of guilt-producing "if only's": *If only I hadn't let myself be alone with him . . . If only I hadn't dressed in a way that turned him on . . . If only I hadn't led him on . . . If only I hadn't been sexually aroused as he assaulted me . . . If only I hadn't cooperated with him. . . .*

Listen carefully: If you've been sexually assaulted, *you didn't cause it, and it's not your fault!* You don't need to feel guilty. You are the victim, not the offender.

You may feel guilty because you dressed or acted in ways which turned him on. You may have permitted him some freedom in petting that made you uncomfortable. You may have cooperated in some way or even been sexually aroused. But if he took sex from you without your permission, you've been raped. Nothing you did told him it was okay to rape you. You are the victim of a crime, and it's not your fault.

Another reason you may feel guilty is because you are emotionally aware that you have been involved in a wrong. Sex is a beautiful experience which God designed to be enjoyed by husband and wife. Since that isn't how you experienced it, you may subconsciously feel that you are an accessory to the great wrong which occurred. The problem is that you are confusing yourself with the offender. You didn't commit the wrong; you *were wronged*. It's not your fault. You no longer need to feel guilty.

Another reason you may struggle with guilt is from other people who blame you for getting raped. They say, either directly or indirectly, "Nice girls don't get raped; only loose girls do. If you were a nice girl running around with nice men, this wouldn't have happened to you." Or they imply that you wouldn't have been raped if your Christian faith had been stronger. God was obviously punishing you for being a weak Christian.

The fact is that all kinds of women, regardless of their socioeconomic position, age, physical appearance, or level of spiritual maturity, get raped. No matter what you did, what you didn't do, or what you could have done, you are the victim. It's not your fault.

"It couldn't have happened to me." Many women can't believe that someone they know could have raped them. The idea is too painful. And so emotionally they attempt to bury the episode in their subconscious and deny that it happened. They tell themselves, "It wasn't rape. It couldn't have been rape. He wasn't some stranger abducting me at gunpoint. He was my boyfriend. Rapes don't happen between boyfriend and girlfriend."

One reason you may be tempted to deny that you were raped is because acquaintance rapes are so seldom mentioned. It may be happening to other girls you know or other female students on your campus. But you're not aware of it because these girls aren't talking about it. So when it happened to you, you may have been tempted to call it "a problem with our relationship" or otherwise deny that you were raped.

The problem with denial is that the problem and all its attending emotions get buried instead of healed. Since they are not brought to the surface and resolved, the memories and hurts continue to fester inside, causing additional pain and keeping the traumatic event alive. In order to move from victim to survivor, date rape needs to be identified for what it is, brought to the surface, and dealt with, as we shall discuss in the next chapter.

"I'm so afraid." Fear, especially related to being with men, is a natural response to a date rape experience. Some victims are suddenly afraid of being with any man, being alone, or living alone. If the assailant was tall, the victim will often fear any tall man she meets. If he had a mustache, she may be fearful of any man with a mustache. Even the scent of the cologne worn by the rapist may cause the victim to fear another man wearing that brand of cologne.

Some women are afraid that their assailant will attack again. One survey noted that 41 percent of raped women expect to get raped again.[16] As a result, they enroll in self-defense courses. They change their telephone number. They install additional door locks. They sleep with the lights on or move in with a friend. When the fear which accompanies date rape is not dealt with, it may grow into a serious problem affecting all the victim's future relationships with men, even her husband.

"I feel worthless." Many victims of date rape sense a deep inner hurt and dismay which causes them to see themselves as "damaged goods." They feel dirty, used, and abused. Their self-image is bruised, and they wonder if they will ever be worth anything again. One study revealed that 30 percent of the rape victims surveyed contemplated suicide after the incident, 31 percent sought psychotherapy, and 82 percent said that the experience had permanently changed them.[17]

If you have experienced a sense of worthlessness and hopelessness as a result of your victimization, your feelings are normal and natural. You have been abused and violated, and your self-image may be temporarily distorted. But you are not worthless. Your value to God and others has not changed. That's why we suggest you consider getting professional help as you work through this trauma. If these emotions are not dealt with, they can lead to depression and sometimes even to despair. As you go through the healing process, your self-perception can be restored.

Social Responses to Date Rape

Date rape can really upset your social life. You may find that some people avoid you. Why? Because they don't know what to say to the victim of date rape. So they stay away in order to avoid the discomfort they feel being around you.

Your social involvement—or lack of involvement—may be governed by your fear that everyone knows you've been raped. You may find yourself tempted to stay home instead of being with your friends. You may not want to go anywhere unless you have a trusted friend along. You may feel like cutting classes or not going to work because of the stares or questions you will get, or because you are uncertain how to act around others. You may want to refuse all dates with men, fearing anything close to a sexual situation.

Your hesitancy in relationships with friends or strangers is a normal response to your victimization. Chances are this has never happened to you before. You aren't prepared for how you should act around people or for how they will act around you.

Ironically, it's the support you receive from your family and friends which will be the most helpful element in your recovery. If you pull away from them, you are only hurting yourself. As we shall see in the next chapter, your willingness to let others help you is an important key to your healing.

Spiritual Responses to Date Rape

If you are the victim of date rape and a Christian, it probably didn't take you long to start asking some of the following questions: Where was God when I was being assaulted? Did He know what was happening to me? Did He care? Did this happen to me because God isn't loving or powerful enough to stop it? The Bible says, "The good man does not escape all troubles—he has them too. But the Lord helps him in each and every one" (Psalm 34:19, TLB). We can't escape evil that exists in the world, but we have a hope that God does help us even at those traumatic times in our life.

Have you voiced questions like these to God or to others? It's a normal response, especially if your date rape experience is the first major trauma in your life. God isn't threatened by your doubts. In fact, your honest questions give Him room to help you begin to understand how He is able to redeem even the tragedies of our lives. He may not answer all your questions at once. But just remain open to Him and continue communicating your feelings to Him. Psalm 62:8 says, "Tell him all your problems" (ICB). You will eventually discover that He didn't cause or choose for you to be raped. What happened to you is the result of man's sinfulness and Satan's desire to "steal and kill and destroy" (John 10:10). For some reason God allowed you to be wounded, just as He allowed His own Son to die a cruel death on the cross. But He is present now to restore you and heal you. Psalm 147:3 says, "He heals the broken-hearted. He bandages their wounds" (ICB).

CHAPTER FIVE

How Can I Survive Date Rape?

Knowing what she knows now, Jamie would give anything to relive the weeks up to the Spring Formal—and do it differently. At first, she torments herself with thoughts of how she should have dressed, talked, and acted around Todd. She wishes she would have been more decisive about setting limits for her physical relationship with Todd and more direct about communicating those limits. Eventually Jamie realizes it is futile to think about all the "what if's", but she's not sure what she can do to put her life back together.

Todd struggles with regret too. He isn't quite sure how his passions got the best of him or why he kept going after Jamie resisted him. But he knows now that he was out of control, and he wishes he could go back and undo what he did. He feels terrible, but he doesn't know what to do about it.

If you've been the victim of date rape, you know the helpless feeling of wanting to change the past but being unable to do so. You wish it had never happened. You wish you could go back and erase it or do it differently. But unless the time machines we read about in science fiction novels somehow become a reality, you'll only be able to deal with the past as it impacts the present and the future. If you dwell on the past, you will continue to be a victim of that tragic event. But if you learn to deal with your victimization today and in the days ahead, you will become a survivor instead of a victim and find the healing that God can provide for you.

In this chapter I will share with you several practical steps for surviving date rape. First, I want to list a number of steps which should be taken immediately after a rape occurs. This is important information you need to have in case you or a friend are raped in the future. Second, I'll outline the stages of the long-term healing process you need to experience to survive date rape. Third, I want to talk to you about your attitude toward the man who raped you. Finally, I'll address guys who have been perpetrators of date rape. There's hope and healing for them too, and I want to share it with you.

It Just Happened—What Should I Do?

Most rape counselors agree that there are several important things you must do as soon after your rape as possible. If Jamie had called me for advice as soon as she got back to the dorm after her experience with Todd, these are the steps I would have suggested:

1. Talk to someone you trust. You must immediately tell someone what happened to you. But choose that person carefully. It should be someone you know well and deeply trust: your mother or father, a mature sister or brother, a proven Christian girlfriend, your pastor or his wife. You should choose someone whom you know is willing to counsel you, support you, help you, and stand with you through all the difficult days ahead. If such a person is not immediately available, you may want to call a rape crisis hotline for help and information.

I'm amazed at how many victims of rape fail to tell anyone about it. In one study of women who had experienced an act of rape, 42 percent told no one about the assault. These women have many reasons for their silence. Some of them feel they were at fault in some way, and so they fail to identify their experience as rape. Some are afraid of retaliation from the offender. Some feel that reporting a rape will result in others questioning their character. Some just want to avoid the hassles of dealing with police, doctors, attorneys, and campus officials. Others may question whether anyone will really believe them.

But the personal cost of remaining silent may be far greater than the pain or inconvenience you encounter from speaking out. As described in chapter 4, burying such a traumatic experience inside you may result in emotional and physical problems that can plague you for years: unresolved fear, anger, or mistrust leading to substance abuse, compulsive behavior, physical ailments, broken relationships, even suicide. Save yourself the pain and grief; tell someone about your rape right away.

2. Seek medical attention. You may be in shock immediately after the rape and unaware of some of the physical injuries you have suffered. Ask a friend or relative to take you to your physician, a hospital emergency room, or an urgent-care clinic for a checkup. Most experts recommend that you not shower or douche before seeing a doctor, because valuable evidence for identifying your attacker could be lost. Also, tests for pregnancy and sexually transmitted diseases are necessary to determine future treatment.

3. Decide about reporting the rape to police. You need to understand that filing a police report may lead to an investigation, an arrest, and legal proceedings involving the man you were with. It may be difficult for you to decide to press charges against someone you know. But remember: He committed a crime. He assaulted you physically and forced you into unwanted sexual intercourse. He needs to face up to his behavior. Taking legal action may be your only way of ensuring that the offender gets help before he victimizes someone else.

4. Find a safe place to recover. You may want to ask a relative or friend to stay with you until you have overcome the initial shock of the attack. You may want to get out of town for a few days of "R and R." Take some time to be with a trusted friend or relative, and let them care for you and encourage you. It's also good to spend time praying alone and with another person for God's direction in your recovery process.

5. Plan to seek counseling. You've had a traumatic experience. It will take time for you to work through all the inner hurts and negative feelings which follow such an attack. It's a good idea to find a counselor to help you through the healing process. True, God is able to heal you completely without any assistance from counselors. But He often uses other people in the healing process. I suggest you look for a professional Christian counselor who understands victimization. If

such a person isn't available to you, look for
a minister or dedicated Christian layperson
who has gained some knowledge and insight
on victimization from books or seminars. Set
up a schedule for meeting with this person
regularly.

The Initial Shock Has Passed—
What Do I Do Now?

In her book *A Door of Hope* (Here's Life
Publishers), licensed Christian counselor Jan
Frank lists ten steps of healing God took her
through in her own recovery from sexual
abuse. I want to borrow her list and apply it
to the long-term healing process faced by
women who have been date raped. Notice
that the first letters of each of the steps forms
the acronym, "Free to Care."

1. F-ace the problem. Don't bury it
inside or pretend it didn't happen. You were
raped. You were the victim of a crime. To call
it anything less than what it was will short-
circuit your healing process. If you find yourself unable to tell someone you've been raped,
you are not facing the problem.

You may say, "But doesn't the Bible
instruct us to forget what is behind us and
press on to what is ahead?" (Philippians
3:13–14). Yes, but that doesn't mean you
should ignore the fact that you were raped. In
the preceding verses Paul *does* recount his

sinful past, then urges, "Don't dwell or wallow in the past in such way that it prevents you from moving on toward God's goals for your life." Face your problem honestly and openly for the purpose of dealing with it and moving on.

2. R-ecount the incident. The most direct method of facing the problem I know is to talk to someone about it and seek the help you need for overcoming it. In addition to telling a trusted friend, relative, or counselor about what happened, you may find it helpful to describe in writing your thoughts and feelings about it. Consider keeping a daily journal during your recovery period. It will serve as a personal record of God's healing activity in your life.

3. E-xperience the feelings. Your emotions have probably been on a roller coaster ride ever since you were raped. You may have been tempted to suppress feelings like anger, helplessness, hatred, fear, embarrassment, or the desire for revenge because you thought they were wrong or evil. Feelings are amoral; they're not right or wrong, good or bad. They are merely a God-given inner warning system indicating that something isn't quite right. How you respond to your feelings is the issue. For example, if you feel hatred toward the man who assaulted you, that's normal. It takes time to process our feelings. If you allow that feeling of hatred to totally consume you, that's crippling. People get in trouble if they hold in their feelings. Even the Bible speaks of this in Matthew 18:15, "If your brother sins against you, go and tell him what he did wrong. Do this in private. If he listens to you, then you have helped him to be your brother again" (ICB). Notice that Jesus allows us to experience and acknowledge our feelings.

Don't deny your feelings. Acknowledge them. Describe them thoroughly in your journal. Tell your counselor about them. But base your actions on what God wants you to do, not what you feel like doing. "Give all your worries to him, because he cares for you" (ICB).

4. E-stablish responsibility. Remember: No matter how much you may have provoked your attacker through your actions or dress, you did not ask to be raped. You have been criminally victimized. It's not your fault.

5. T-race behavioral difficulties/ symptoms. As you progress through the weeks and months of your recovery, notice if you are having any problems which may be related to the attack. Are you more anti-social than usual? Are you afraid of men? Are you more self-conscious or easily embarrassed? These problems may be a tip-off that you have some unresolved, hidden attitudes or fears from your experience. Ask God to reveal the areas that still need His healing touch. Talk to your counselor about them, and work together toward resolving them.

6. O-bserve others; educate yourself. Many date rape victims are helped by talking with other women who have been victimized. You may want to spend some time with a support group of rape victims. Or it may be more helpful for you to find a group of godly women who will provide a nurturing atmosphere for you and support you in your spiritual growth during your recovery. Books and tapes on inner healing and related topics are another good resource for education and growth.

7. C-onfront the aggressor. You're not doing your attacker any favors by letting him off the hook. If he is not confronted with his crime, he may repeat it. If you report the attack to police, the legal system will take the lead in confronting him. If you elect to confront him personally, do so only after much prayer and counsel and in a safe environment.

8. A-cknowledge forgiveness. This is such an important and difficult step for many victims of date rape that I want to talk about it more fully in the next section of the chapter.

9. R-ebuild self-image and relationships. You may have been hurt by people who blamed you for causing the rape. You may be plagued by self-doubt and feelings of worthlessness. You need to counter these attacks on your self-image by looking at yourself the way God sees you. The greatest resource for rebuilding your self-image is the Bible. Spend time in God's Word reviewing His unconditional love for you. As your confidence in God's love is restored, you will be able to restore relationships which may have been strained or broken as a result of your date rape.

10. E-xpress concern and empathize with others. As you move through the healing process, don't be surprised if God brings you into contact with other women who have been victimized and who need encouragement and support. Be ready to share your healing experience with those who are just starting out on the road to recovery.

Forgive Him? Are You Kidding?

If you'd have told Jamie a few days after the attack that she needed to forgive Todd for raping her, she probably would have laughed in your face. "How could I forgive him?" you might hear her say. "He did the most unspeakable things to me. I trusted him, and he violated that trust. I don't think I can ever forgive him." If you're a victim like Jamie, perhaps you have harbored the same feelings.

Forgiveness involves letting go of our rights to be angry, bitter, and resentful to the person who has wronged us. It's like tearing up an I.O.U. for a huge sum of money. The reason we can do this is because we know that Jesus has already paid for that sin against us. You are now free to release the feelings and attitudes that plague you.

Don't equate forgiving with forgetting. You won't forget what happened to you any more than you will forget a car accident you were involved in, the death of a loved one, or any other traumatic event in your life. But when you forgive the man who attacked you, you allow God to free you from that memory's power to torment you.

Forgiveness is first an act of the will. It may take a while for your feelings to catch up with your decision, but eventually they will. Don't wait to *feel* like forgiving before you forgive. Sometimes we have to *will* to forgive before the feelings are actually there. Your decision to forgive the man does not depend on him asking for forgiveness. Jesus forgave us on the cross centuries before we repented of our sins (Romans 5:8). There will be a point in time when you will have to decide about forgiving the person who raped you.

The Bible has a lot to say about forgiveness. Even though it will take some time to come to this point, this is where God wants to eventually lead us. Jesus said, "When you stand praying, if you hold anything against anyone, forgive him, so that your Father in heaven may forgive your sins" (Mark 11:25). Paul wrote, "Be kind and compassionate to one another, forgiving each other, just as in Christ God forgave you" (Ephesians 4:32); "Bear with each other and forgive whatever grievances you may have against one another. Forgive as the Lord forgave you" (Colossians 3:13).

Putting your decision to forgive in writing will help to crystallize the attitude of forgiveness in your heart. Write it in your journal or diary. For example, you might simply write something like, "(Name), I forgive you for raping me (date and location)." Or you may want to write a much more detailed expression of forgiveness, itemizing all the physical and emotional wounds you suffered.

A Message to Offenders

If you are a young single man in the sixteen to twenty-four age group, and even higher, you are in the prime category of potential date rape perpetrators. Yes, limited studies suggest that your chances of being involved in sexual aggression are fewer if you are a Christian with a strong moral foundation. But guys, no matter how long you've been a Christian, you're not above being tempted to sexual aggression—especially when the two of you are parked beside a moonlit cove in the middle of the night!

Maybe you've pushed a girl to go farther than she wanted to go sexually, perhaps having intercourse with her against her wishes. If you are guilty of forcing a girl sexually, you probably wouldn't be reading this unless you were interested in trying to make things right. You may be suffering a good deal of hurt yourself as you think about what you did. Your feelings of remorse are a good sign. If you're really serious about turning your life around, here are some steps to help you.

1. Get straight with God. Your offense against the woman you raped was first a sin against God. So your first step toward getting things right is to confess your sin to God and receive His forgiveness. Confession simply means to say the same thing about your sin that God does: that it was sin. When you agree with God that what you did was sin, God is free to cleanse you of your sin (1 John 1:9).

I suggest that you sit down with a blank sheet of paper and write a letter of confession to God. Then seek out a pastor to support you in prayer and hold you accountable spiritually during this time of repentance and healing. Read together Scriptures which remind you of God's forgiveness and restoration. Then pray together and thank God for cleansing you from your sin.

2. Seek counseling and turn your life around. Confession is important, but it's not enough. You must also change your behavior so you don't repeat the offense. This is called *repentance*. To repent literally means to stop going in the direction you're going, turn around, and head in a new direction. If you don't turn your life around, your confession is meaningless.

The best way I know for you to turn around is to seek professional Christian counseling. You need to commit yourself to a counselor who is skilled in working with sex offenders. He will help you deal with the root of your problem. This step may take several months, a year, or more. But stay with it. Unless you expose and treat the underlying causes of your offense, you are likely to repeat it in the future.

3.   Confess to the victim and, if necessary, to the authorities. At some point in the counseling process, ask your counselor to help you decide the best way to apologize to the woman you raped. For example, you may decide to write a letter confessing plainly what you did, expressing your sorrow over it, and explaining the steps you are pursuing in order to change. Clearly state that you were at fault, not her. Even if you feel she acted or dressed in a way which led you on, focus on *your* wrong behavior.

In your letter you may also want to offer to make restitution. For example, you can pay for the victim's counseling, doctor bills, and personal property damaged in the assault (clothing, jewelry, other items). Offer to do whatever you can to help her feel that she has been justly compensated.

If the victim elects to press charges against you, you may end up facing punishment at the hands of the court. Be entirely truthful and cooperative with the police, attorneys, judge, and other officials. Alert them that you are already in counseling for your problem. Pray for God's grace and mercy to attend your case, but be ready to pay the penalty for your crime.

4. Pray for reconciliation. When the offender's confession, repentance, and restitution are met with the victim's forgiveness, reconciliation is possible. This doesn't mean that your relationship with the victim will return to where it was before the attack. It may take years before the woman can even speak to you, let alone have any kind of a relationship with you. But if you have done your part wholeheartedly, at least your conscience will be clear and the possibility of a reconciled relationship is real.

Does the story of Jamie and Todd have a happy ending? Not hardly, not anything close to what it could have been.

It was about 2:00 A.M. when Jamie returned to her dorm after the Spring Formal. Her roommate had gone home for the weekend, so Jamie sat alone in her dark room crying. At about 5:00 she called Tanya, a Christian faculty member at the college who also sponsors the campus fellowship group. Tanya encouraged Jamie to advise the college career pastor of the incident. Jamie and Tanya had become close through the group, and Jamie felt Tanya was the one to go with her to talk to the pastor.

After talking with the pastor, Tanya and Jamie went to the emergency room at the city hospital. Jamie didn't really want to go. She was embarrassed and hurt. She didn't want to explain to strangers what had happened to her. But Tanya had attended a rape crisis seminar and knew the importance of Jamie receiving medical treatment right away. Jamie was treated for a couple of minor abrasions and a slightly sprained wrist. Tanya took Jamie back to the dorm where she picked up some clean clothes and her overnight bag. Then they went to Tanya's apartment, where Jamie finally fell asleep.

Todd got home at about 3:00 A.M. but couldn't go to sleep. The seriousness of his actions washed over him in dark, suffocating waves. He had failed Jamie and he had failed God. But the most frightening thing was that he had lost control of himself and didn't know why. He picked up the phone several times to call Jamie, but hung up each time before dialing her number.

By 10:30 Todd was so distraught and confused that he had to do something. Finally he drove over to see Keith, the associate pastor at the church he and Jamie had been attending. Keith had always been friendly and approachable to Todd. They had gotten together a few times to shoot hoops and split a pizza. Todd felt that if anyone could help him understand what he had done and deal with it, Keith could. They ended up spending most of Saturday together in Keith's study.

Over the next few days, Jamie had to decide about filing a police report charging Todd with rape. This was a difficult decison for her. She decided to get ongoing professional Christian counseling to help her work through all this. Jamie finished the spring term at Campbell, but did her best to avoid contact with Todd. Todd began attending another church, on the advice of the pastor, so that Jamie could get the help she needed from the church.

Two days before going home for the summer, Jamie received a letter from Todd. He apologized for what he had done. He told Jamie he had begun a long-term counseling/ discipling relationship with Keith in hopes of coming to terms with himself and his behavior and turning his life around. He wished Jamie a good summer.

The following year, Todd and Jamie ran into each other on campus a few times.

They spoke briefly about superficial topics. On their last meeting Todd summoned his courage to tell Jamie in person how sorry he was for what had happened. He was relieved to hear Jamie say, "I accept your apology, Todd, and I forgive you." They parted and never saw each other again.

Perhaps you are reading this book in time to help you avoid this kind of not-so-happy ending in your dating relationships. I hope so. I pray that you will take the suggestions in these pages to heart and commit yourself to help prevent date rape from happening to you and your friends.

If you have already been involved in date rape, I hope you now see yourself as a survivor instead of just a victim. Our God is a God of hope and healing. Jeremiah 30:17 says, "I will bring back your health. And I will heal your injuries, says the Lord" (ICB).

Because we're His child, Jesus Christ has promised to help us. John 16:33 says, "In this world you will have trouble. But be brave! I have defeated the world" (ICB). Thanks to Him, there are still happy endings.

This book is the companion book to the thirty-minute video entitled "It Can Happen to You." If you are using the video as part of a youth event, we suggest providing this book to each one in the group. If you do not have the video, you may obtain it at your local Christian bookstore or by calling Josh McDowell Ministry's fulfillment house at 1–800–222–5674 (credit card orders only by phone).

Date rape and sexual abuse is devastating. Someone in your group may have been abused or know of someone who has been. The video may open up some deep wounds and feelings, so it will be important to have a number of these books on hand. Explain that after the showing of the video they can get the book from you.

Following your showing of the video, you will also want to have a time for discussion on how to help prevent date rape. On the next page, we have prepared some questions for group interaction.

Rape and sexual abuse has far-reaching emotional and psychological ramifications in a person's life. If you sense, or know, that one of your youth has been sexually abused, you may want to seek professional and legal advice on how to proceed with dealing with them. There are a number of excellent Christian groups and counselors that can give you guidance.

VIDEO DISCUSSION
QUESTIONS

1. God's Word says to avoid sexual immorality (1 Thessalonians 4:3) because God wants to provide for us and to protect us from damaging consequences. But what if a person is forced to be sexually involved against their will—is that person guilty of wrong doing?

   [Answer: A person who is forced to be involved sexually is the victim and is not in any way at fault or guilty of wrong.]

2. Does a girl ever "owe it" to a guy to give out sexually? Why?

   [Answer: No—absolutely not. No matter how much a guy has spent on the girl or how long they have dated, sex is *never* to be seen as payment or reward.]

3. What are some steps you can take to help avoid date rape?

   [Answer: (1) Avoid "blind dates."
   (2) Group date.
   (3) Plan your dates.
   (4) Avoid isolated situations or places on your dates.
   (5) Set your standards ahead of time and communicate them clearly.]

4. Ask your group to list at least 5 dating standards they have or want to set for themselves that will help reduce the risk of date rape.

   Explain that you have this book available and offer it to each one in your group. Tell them if they have any further questions about "date rape" or forming their dating standards you would be glad to help them find the answers. Close in prayer.

Sex, Guilt, and Forgiveness, by Josh McDowell (Tyndale House Publishers).

A Door of Hope, by Jan Frank (Here's Life Publishers).

Building Your Self-Image, by Josh McDowell (Tyndale House Publishers).

Teenage Q & A Book, by Josh McDowell and Bill Jones (Word Publishing).

Friend of the Lonely Heart, by Josh McDowell and Norm Wakefield (Word Publishing).

Dating: Picking and Being a Winner, Josh McDowell, editor; Bill Jones and Barry St. Clair (Here's Life Publishers).

ADDITIONAL RESOURCES
BY JOSH MCDOWELL

Books

How to Be a Hero to Your Kids (Josh McDowell and Dick Day)
How to Help Your Child Say "No" to Sexual Pressure
Unlocking the Secrets of Being Loved, Accepted, and Secure (Josh McDowell and Dale Bellis)
Love, Dad

Video

How to Be a Hero to Your Kids (Josh McDowell and Dick Day)
It Can Happen to You
Friend of the Lonely Heart (Josh McDowell and Norm Wakefield)
WHY WAIT? Video Collection:
  Why Waiting Is Worth the Wait
  God Is No Cosmic Kill-joy
  How to Handle the Pressure Lines
  A Clean Heart for a New Start
Evidence for Faith Series
How to Help Your Child Say "No" to Sexual Pressure
Let's Talk about Love and Sex
The Myths of Sex Education
"No!"—The Positive Answer
Where Youth Are Today
Who Do You Listen To?

Audio

How to Be a Hero to Your Kids (Josh McDowell and Dick Day)
Friend of the Lonely Heart (Josh McDowell and Norm Wakefield)
The Teenage Q&A Book on Tape
Why Wait? What You Need to Know about the Teen Sexuality Crisis (Josh McDowell and Dick Day)
How to Help Your Child Say "No" to Sexual Pressure
"No!"—The Positive Answer (Love Waiting music)
The Secret of Loving
Why Waiting Is Worth the Wait

16 mm Films

Evidence for Faith Series
Messianic Prophecy
Misconceptions about Christianity, Part I
Misconceptions about Christianity, Part II
The Reliability of Scripture
A Skeptic's Quest
The Uniqueness of the Bible
Where Youth Are Today: What You Need to Know about the Teen Sexuality Crisis

Available from your Christian bookstore or Word Publishing

1. Adapted from two studies:

(A) Kanin, E.J., and Parcell, S.R. (1977). "Sexual Aggression: A Second Look at the Offended Female." *Archives of Sexual Behavior*, 6, pp. 67–76.

(B) Charlene L. Muehlenhard and Melany A. Linton, Texas A & M University, "Date Rape and Sexual Aggression in Dating Situations: Incidence and Risk Factors," *Journal of Counseling Psychology*, 1987, Vol. 34, No. 2, p. 189.

2. The Center for the Prevention and Control of Rape teamed Ms. Magazine and Mary P. Koss, Ph. D., Kent State University, for this study. As reported in *I Never Called It Rape—The Ms. Report on Recognizing, Fighting, and Surviving Date and Acquaintance Rape*, by Robin Warshaw, Ms. Foundation/Sara Lazin Books, Harper and Row, New York, 1988.; and in *Violence in Dating Relationships—Emerging Social Issues*, edited by Maureen A. Pirog-Good and Jan E. Stets, Praeger Publishers a division of Greenwood Press Inc., New York, 1989.

3. As reported in *Violence in Dating Relationships*.

4. Dr. Mary P. Koss, as reported in "Date Rape: When Sex Is a Weapon," the Orange County Sexual Assault Network (OSCAN).

5. Ideas and Trends, "The Rape Laws Change Faster Than Perceptions," by Laura Mansnerus, *The New York Times*, 19 February 1989.

6. "Stranger and Acquaintance Rape—Are There Differences In the Victim's Experience?" by Mary P. Koss, Thomas E. Dinero, and Cynthia

A. Seibel, Kent State University, *Psychology of Women Quarterly*, 1988, 12, pp. 6–13.

7. Gerard Waggett, "A Plea to the Soaps: Let's Stop Turning Rapists into Heroes," *TV Guide*, May 27, 1989.

8. As reported in "Distorted Attitudes Reinforced" by Claude Lewis, a *Philadelphia Inquirer* columnist.

9. Ibid.

10. "Date/Acquaintance Rape: What You Need to Know . . ." from the Rape Crisis Center of the Center for Women's Study and Service.

11. Skelton, C.A. (1982), "Situational and Personological Correlates of Sexual Victimization in College Women." Unpublished doctoral dissertation, Auburn University, Alabama. As reported in Barry R. Burkhart and Annette L. Stanton, "Sexual Aggression in Acquaintance Relationships," in *Violence in Intimate Relationships*, Gordon W. Russell, PMA Press, Great Neck, NY, 1988, p. 45.

12. As reported in "Date Rape: When Sex Is a Weapon."

13. Kanin, E.J. (1957). "Male Aggression in Dating-Courtship Relations." *American Journal of Sociology, 10*, pp. 197–204.

14. Koss, M.P. (1985). "The Hidden Rape Victim: Personality, Attitudinal, and Situational Characteristics." *Psychology of Women Quarterly*, 9, pp. 193–212.

15. As reported in *Violence in Dating Relationships*.

16. Ibid.

17. Ibid.

LET'S STAY -IN- TOUCH !

If you have grown personally as a result of this material, we should stay in touch. You will want to continue in your Christian growth, and to help your faith become even stronger, our team is constantly developing new materials.

We are now publishing a monthly newsletter called 5 Minutes with Josh which will

1) tell you about those new materials as they become available
2) answer your tough questions
3) give creative tips on being an effective parent
4) let you know our ministry needs
5) keep you up to date on my speaking schedule (so you can pray).

If you would like to receive this publication, simply fill out the coupon below and send it in. By special arrangement 5 Minutes with Josh will come to you regularly — no charge.

Let's keep in touch!

Josh

☐ **Yes!** I want to receive the free subscription to **5 Minutes with JOSH**

_____
NAME

_____
ADDRESS

_____
CITY, STATE/ZIP

SLC-2024

Mail To:
Josh McDowell
c/o 5 Minutes with Josh
Campus Crusade for Christ
Arrowhead Springs
San Bernardino, CA 92414